Building Blocks Sampler Quilt

Quilting for Beginners
Quilt Pattern & Tutorial

Felicity Walker

Sign up for Felicity's free newsletter at
QuiltersDiary.com

COPYRIGHT © 2016 FELICITY WALKER
All rights reserved.

ISBN: 1533005729
ISBN-13: 978-1533005724

Felicity Walker

Contents

Building Blocks Sampler Quilt……………………………………..4

1/ One Easy Quilt Sampler…12 Essential Blocks ….5

2/ Tools and Fabric………………………………………………….6

3/ Piecing Basics ……………………………………………………9

4/ Four-Patch Block………………………………………………..11

5/ Nine-Patch Blocks……………………………………………..12

6/ Rail Fence Block……………………………………………….13

7/ Half-Square Triangle Block………………………………14

8/ Pinwheel Block…………………………………………………16

9/ Snowball Block…………………………………………………17

10/ Friendship Star Block……………………………………..18

11/ Spool Block……………………………………………………..20

12/ Diamond-in-a-Square Block……………………………21

13/ Quarter-Square Triangle Block……………………….23

14/ Three-Quarter-Square Block 25

15/ Quilt Construction: Adding Sashing..................26

16/ Quilt Construction: Adding Borders 28

17/ Quilt Construction: Finishing the Quilt 30

18/ Conclusion..32

19/ About Felicity Walker..33

Felicity Walker

Building Blocks Sampler Quilt
38" x 48½" (96.5 cm x 123 cm)

1/ One Easy Quilt Sampler... Twelve Blocks You Can Use to Make Endless Quilts

THIS LITTLE BOOK includes a complete pattern for a twelve-block sampler quilt. It also includes patterns for the twelve easy blocks that make up the sampler.

You will also learn how to add sashing and borders to give your quilt visual harmony.

Twelve Building Blocks Every Quilter Should Know

There's a good reason why I call these twelve easy blocks the building blocks of quilting. Once you have them in your quilter's tool kit, you can use them to create literally hundreds of different quilts.

Every one of these blocks is a workhorse that you will find in many, many quilt patterns. You will see many of them as the basic components of larger and more complicated quilt blocks. They all add a sense of life and movement to a quilt. Even better, they are all simple enough for you to sew successfully, even if you've never made a quilt before.

And all twelve blocks have a finished size of nine inches. This is a standard size that is much used in quilt patterns. You can easily mix and match these blocks with each other or with other blocks to make your own quilt patterns. In fact, you can use this pattern as a framework for many different quilts, just replacing the sampler blocks with your own selections.

Need Help with Quilting Techniques?

The pattern in this book is a companion to my book for new quilters, *Quilts for Beginners*, which covers in detail all the tools, supplies, and techniques you need to successfully make your first quilts. If you need help with such things as how to cut your fabric, how to sew a 1/4" seam, how to baste a quilt, or exactly how to put on the binding, check out *Quilts for Beginners*. It covers everything you need to know.

2/ Tools and Fabric

You will need a few basic quilting tools to make this sampler:

- Sewing machine with a good straight stitch
- Rotary cutter
- Cutting mat
- See-through cutting ruler
- Seam ripper
- Scissors
- Iron and pressing surface
- Basting spray
- Blue painter's tape
- Good-quality quilting thread in a coordinating color

Fabric Requirements

The 12 blocks for this quilt are made from three fabrics: a solid white, a red print, and an aqua print. For the sashing and borders, I used an understated gray print. The binding is made from the same red print used for the blocks and sashing cornerstones. This chart shows shows how much of each fabric you will need:

(white)	1 yard
(red)	1 yard (includes binding)
(aqua)	¼ yard
(gray)	1¼ yard
Backing fabric	3-1/8 yards
Batting	Lap quilt size, or one piece at least 41" x 52"

Building Blocks Sampler Quilt

Cutting Requirements

If you want to cut all the fabric for the whole quilt at once, this page shows you exactly what to cut.

(white)	• One 3 ½" x 9 ½" strip • Fifteen 3½" squares • Eight 4" squares • Four 5" squares • Two 6" squares • Three 10 ¼" squares	(teal)	• One 3½" x 9 ½" strip • Eight 3½" squares • Two 4" squares • Three 5" squares • One 6" square • One 10" square • Two 10¼" squares
(red)	• Five 2½" strips by full width of the fabric (for the binding) • One 3½" x 9 ½" strip • Six 2" squares • Six 3½" squares • Six 4" squares • One 5" square • One 6" square • One 9½" square • One 10" square • Two 10¼" squares	(gray)	• Seventeen strips 2" x 9½" each • Two strips 4½" x 41" • Two strips 4½" x 39"
Backing fabric	One or two pieces measuring 41" x 52", depending on fabric width. See Chapter 17.	Batting	Lap quilt size, or one piece at least 41" x 52"

These quantities assume that you optimize your use of each fabric by piecing shorter strips into longer strips as needed.

They also assume that the usable width of your fabric yardage is 40", after you remove the selvage edges. Your fabric may be a little wider, depending on the manufacturer.

Tips on Choosing Fabrics

Use smaller-scale prints. Most of the blocks in this quilt are made from fairly small squares and triangles. Because of that, I recommend using prints with small-scale patterns, so the pattern doesn't get lost when you cut up the fabric.

Avoid directional prints. The quilt is easiest to make if you choose prints that look the same from any direction – no stripes or fabrics that look upside-down from certain angles. If you use directional fabrics, you will need more fabric so you can fussy-cut pieces to face in the directions that look good.

Dimensions

All the blocks in the quilt are square, with a finished size of 9" (9½" before they are sewed.) The sashing is 1½" wide finished (2" wide before it is sewed.) The borders are 4" wide when finished (4½" before they are sewed.)

3/ Piecing Basics

ALL THE BLOCKS in this sampler pattern are easy enough for any quilter to make, even if this is your first quilting experience.

Most of the blocks are made by sewing together various combinations of squares and half-square triangles. Chapter 7 gives a detailed tutorial on how to make half-square triangle blocks.

The Diamond-in-a-Square block, Quarter-Square Triangle block, and Three-Quarter-Square Triangle blocks have special instructions, which you will find in the chapters on making those blocks.

To make the rest of the blocks in the sampler, just follow the basic piecing instructions given here.

Basic Piecing Guidelines

- Before you sew any block together, first lay out the pieces on your work surface as they will be arranged in the finished block. Check the layout against the block diagrams in this book to make sure the pieces are in the right order. It's surprisingly easy to get them mixed up, so double-check before you sew!

- Do the same thing when you assemble the blocks into a quilt top: lay out all the blocks first, so you can double-check that you have them arranged the way you want them before you sew.

- Sew all seams with a scant ¼" seam allowance.

- Place pieces with right sides together for sewing.

- Press and square up your block every time you add a new seam.

- In most situations, press seams to the side with the darker fabric, so dark seam allowances don't show through on the finished quilt.

- Sew blocks one row at a time. First sew together all the pieces in the top row, moving from left to right, then the pieces in the next row, until each row is completely sewed together.

- Once all the pieces in each row are sewed together, press and square up each row. Then sew the rows together, working from the top of the block to the bottom.

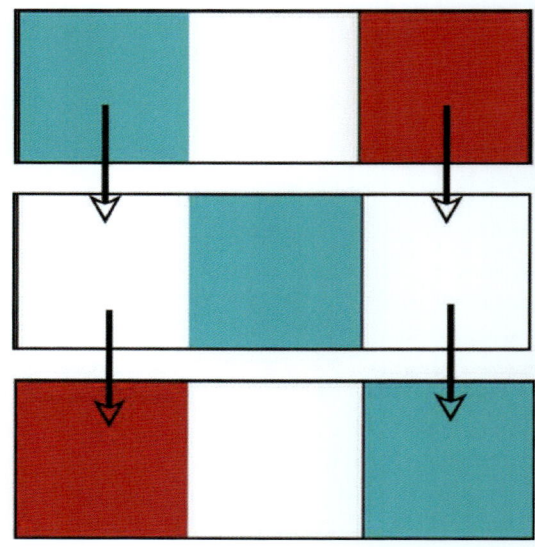

4/ Four-Patch Block

THE COZY CHECKERBOARD look of the Four-Patch quilt block is well known to anyone who spends much time around quilts. Four-patch blocks are used to build many more complex blocks.

To piece the block, follow the basic piecing guidelines in Chapter 3.

Fabric Requirements

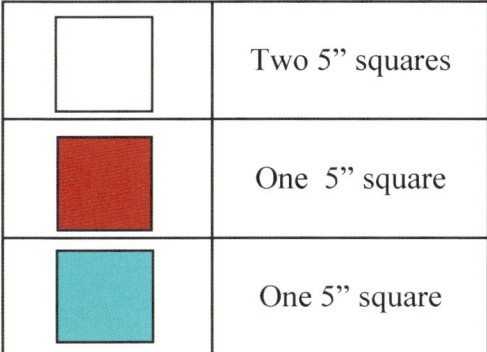

	Two 5" squares
	One 5" square
	One 5" square

5/ Nine-Patch Blocks

Regular nine-patch block

Reverse nine-patch block

A NINE-PATCH QUILT BLOCK is made of nine fabric squares arranged in a checkerboard pattern of alternating lights and darks. The versatile Nine-Patch is one of the basic quilt blocks you will use over and over.

There are two types of Nine-Patch blocks – one with darker squares in all the corners, which I call a regular Nine-Patch block, and one that has lighter squares in the corners. I call this a reverse Nine-Patch. This sampler includes one of each type.

To piece the block, follow the general piecing instructions in Chapter 3.

Fabric Requirements

The requirements shown here will give you enough squares to make both Nine-Patch blocks.

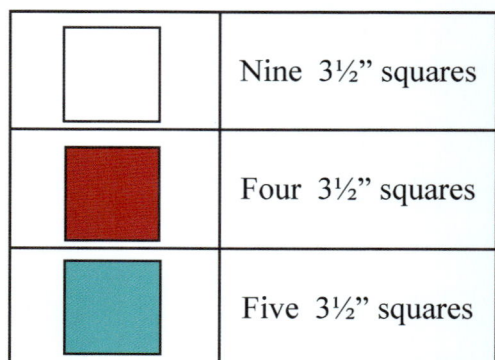

6/ Rail Fence Block

RAIL FENCE MIGHT just be the easiest of all the blocks in this sampler, and that's saying something, because every single block in this quilt is easy to sew.

There are quite a few variations on the Rail Fence block. This one consists of three rectangles sewed together with two straight seams.

To piece the block, just sew the strips together, following the general piecing instructions in Chapter 3.

Fabric Requirements

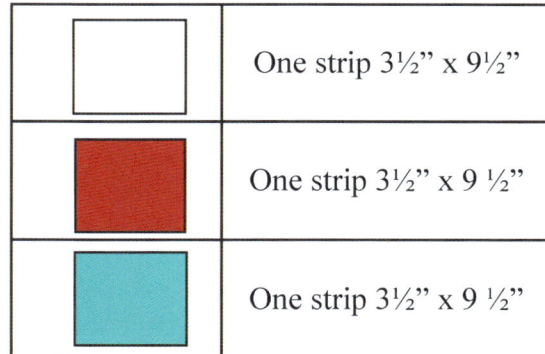

7/ Half-Square Triangle Block

THIS ENDLESSLY USEFUL block is one of the most widely used blocks in quilting. There are a number of different ways to make the block. I show you the simplest one here, which starts with two same-size fabric squares. Each set of two squares makes two identical triangle blocks. You only need one big triangle block for the sampler, so you will have one bonus block to use in another project.

The technique you use to make the big Half-Square Triangle block for the sampler is the same technique you will use to make the smaller triangle blocks that go into many of the other blocks in this pattern.

Fabric Requirements

You will need two 10" squares, one red and one aqua. Using a 10" square will make your block come out a little oversized. You will trim it down to 9½" as a final step after sewing.

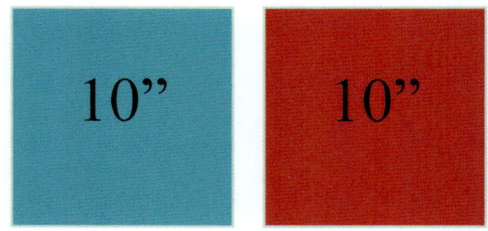

Making Half-Square Triangles

1. Lay the lighter-colored square on your work surface, right side down. Use a ruler and a pencil or fine-point permanent marker to draw a diagonal line from corner to corner across the back of the square. The line won't show when the block is finished.

2. Lay the two squares with right sides together. Align the edges and corners carefully.

3. Sew a seam ¼" away from each side of the line you marked. (If you have a ¼" quilting foot, using it makes this easy.) The dotted yellow lines in the photo represent the lines to sew:

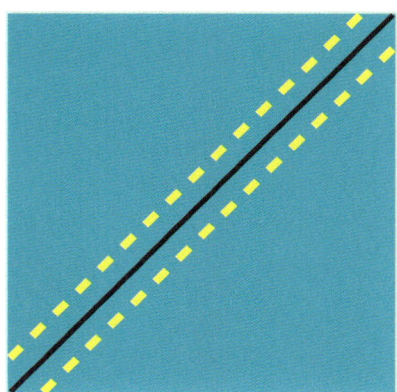

4. Use a ruler and rotary cutter to cut the block in half along the center line. You will get two triangular units:

5. Open the blocks and press the seam allowance to the darker side. You will end up with two mirror-image Half-Square Triangle blocks:

6. The completed blocks will have little tails at two of their corners. Use a ruler and rotary cutter to trim the blocks down to size and cut off the tails. If possible, use a square ruler with a 45-degree line that runs from corner to corner. When you square up the block, align the diagonal line on the ruler with the diagonal seam line on the block. If you don't have a square ruler, use a rectangular one and make sure all four corners of the blocks are square.

8/ Pinwheel Block

The Pinwheel block is one of the simplest blocks based on the ever-useful Half-Square Triangle. I love the way Pinwheel blocks seem to set a quilt spinning with color.

Fabric Requirements

☐ (white)	Two 6"squares
■ (red)	One 6" square
■ (aqua)	One 6" square

Making the Block

The block consists of two sets of Half Square Triangles: one red-and-white set, and one aqua-and-white set.

1. Use the red square and one of the two white squares to make a set of two triangle blocks, following the instructions in Chapter 7.

2. Use the aqua square and the other white square o make a set of two aqua-and-white triangle blocks.

3. Lay out the blocks as shown above, then sew the block together using the general piecing instructions in Chapter 3.

9/ Snowball Block

THIS SLIGHTLY MORE elaborate variation of the basic Snowball quilt block is made from squares and half-square triangle blocks. It's easy and colorful.

Making the Block

1. First, you'll use the 4" white and 4" red squares to make four Half-Square Triangle blocks. The triangle blocks go in the outer corners of the block. Follow the instructions in Chapter 7 for making the Half-Square Triangles, then trim the blocks down to 3½" square.

2. Lay out the block as shown in the diagram above, then follow the general piecing instructions in Chapter 3 to sew the block together.

Fabric Requirements

white	Two 4" squares Four 3½" squares
red	Two 4" squares
teal	One 3½" square

10/ Friendship Star Block

EVERY QUILTER SHOULD have a few star blocks in her bag of tricks. Friendship Star is one of the simplest star blocks you can make. It is also one of my favorites because of its charming pinwheel quality. The block is made by combining a square with Half-Square Triangle blocks.

Making the Block

You will need two different sets of Half-Square Triangle blocks for this block.

1. Use two of the 4" white squares and the two 4" aqua squares to sew four aqua-and-white Half-Square Triangles.

Fabric Requirements

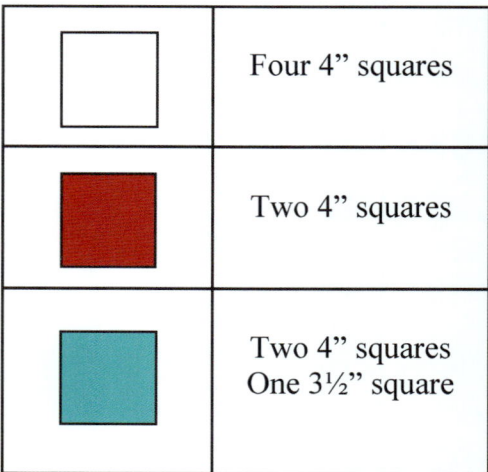

	Four 4" squares
	Two 4" squares
	Two 4" squares One 3½" square

Building Blocks Sampler Quilt

2. Use the two 4" red squares and the remaining two 4" white squares to make four red-and-white half-square triangle blocks.

3. Follow the instructions for making half-square triangles in Chapter 7.

4. Trim all the triangle blocks to 3½" square.

5. Lay out the blocks the way they appear in the Friendship Star block diagram above.

6. Use the general piecing instructions from Chapter 3 to sew the block together.

11/ Spool Block

WHAT BETTER BLOCK for new quilters to make than Spool, which looks so much like a spool of thread? The block is another easy one made by mixing squares with Half-Square Triangle blocks.

Making the Block

1. Use the two 4" white squares and the two 4" red squares to make four triangle blocks, following the instructions in Chapter 7. Trim the blocks to 3½".

2. Arrange the triangle blocks and squares as shown in the Spool block diagram above, then sew the block together using the instructions in Chapter 3.

Fabric Requirements

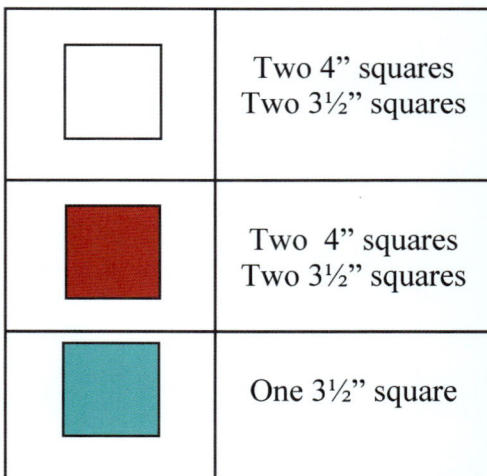

12/ Diamond-in-a-Square Block

THIS BLOCK IS made by sewing four small squares to the corners of a larger square, then trimming off the extra fabric.

Fabric Requirements

(white)	Two 5" squares
(red)	One 9½" square
(aqua)	Two 5" squares

Making the Block

1. Put the white and aqua squares on your work surface, right side down. Draw a diagonal line from corner to corner across each square, like this:

2. Lay the marked aqua squares on top of the red square, with right sides together and corners aligned as shown:

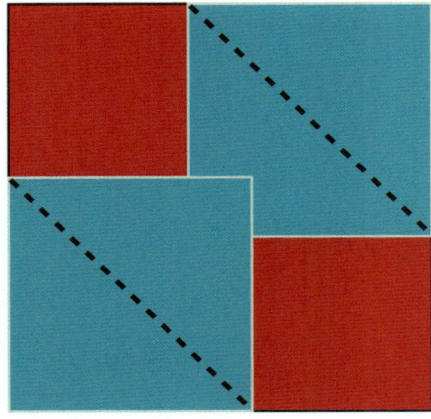

3. Stitch the aqua squares from corner to corner along the dotted lines, then flip the inner corners of the aqua squares over and press them to the outer corners of the block. If you would like, you can trim the corner of the bottom layer to a ¼" seam allowance.

4. Lay the marked white squares on the other two corners of the red square, with right sides together and corners aligned. Sew along the diagonal lines the same way you did with the aqua squares, then press the white squares to the outer corners.

5. If you would like to, you can trim away the under-layers of fabric. This reduces the bulk of the block, but you don't have to do it if you prefer not to.

If you sew all the corner squares on correctly, the tips of the center diamond should be 1/4" away from the outer edge of the block when you are done. The extra rim of fabric may look funny to you, but it means that your block came out perfectly. Once you sew the block into the rest of the quilt, the extra fabric will be hidden and the points of the diamond should just touch the outer edges of the block.

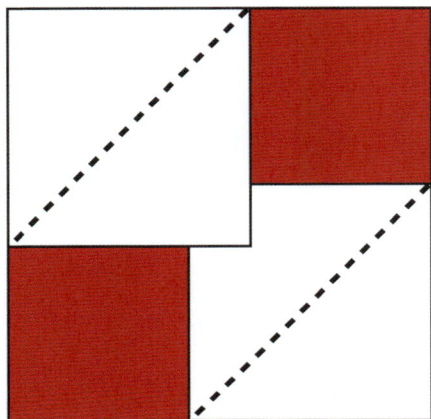

13/ Quarter-Square Triangle Block

THE HOURGLASS SHAPE of the Quarter-Square Triangle blocks give a quilt a symmetrical diagonal energy.

Fabric Requirements

☐	Two 10 ¼" squares
🟥	One 10 ¼" square
🟦	One 10¼" square

Making the Block

1. Lay the two white squares on your work surface, right sides down. Use your ruler to draw two diagonal lines across the back of each block, like this:

2. Lay a white square together with an aqua square, with right sides together. Sew the block from corner to corner, ¼" away from *one* of the lines you drew. Sew on both sides of the line. The red dotted lines in the diagram represent your seams:

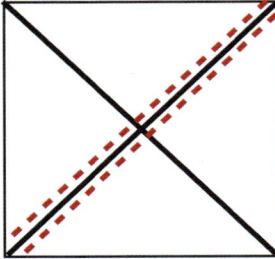

3. Cut the block in two along the line you *didn't* sew:

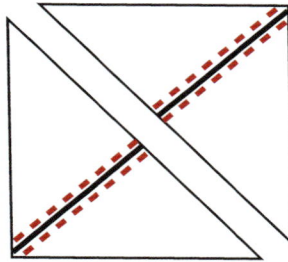

4. Cut the two pieces in half along the line between the two seams. You will end up with four triangular sections that look like this:

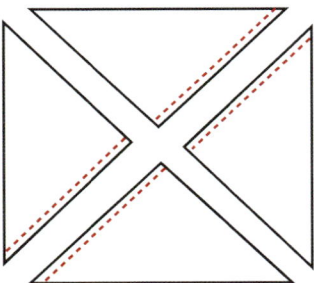

5. Press the four triangles open. They will look something like this:

6. Repeat the same process with the red square and the second white square. You should end up with four red-and-white units similar to the aqua-and-white units.

7. Take one red-and-white unit and one aqua-and-white unit and lay them with right sides together. Make sure the aqua and red sections each face a white section.

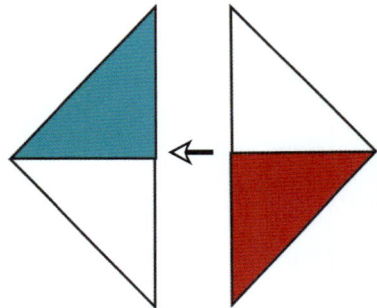

8. Sew the two units together along the long side of the triangle. You should end up with a 9½" square block that looks like the diagram at the beginning of the chapter.

   Tip: you will have an extra red-and-white unit after you make this block. If you're making the complete sampler quilt, you can use the extra unit for the Three-Quarter-Square Triangle block instead of making new quarter-square triangles.

14/ Three-Quarter-Square Triangle Block

THREE-QUARTER-SQUARE TRIANGLE BLOCKS are a clever cross between a Half-Square Triangle and a Quarter-Square Triangle.

Fabric Requirements

	One 10¼" square
	One 10¼" square
	One 10¼" square

Making the Block

1. Make a Quarter-Square Triangle from the aqua and white squares, following the instructions in Chapter 13.

2. Cut the red square diagonally in half. Handle it with care to avoid stretching the cut edge.

3. Lay one of the aqua-and-white triangle units with one of the red half-squares.

4. Sew the two units together along the long side of the triangle.

5. Press the block open and square up. Voila!

15/ Quilt Construction: Adding Sashing

THE STRIPS BETWEEN the blocks in the center of the sampler quilt are called sashing. Sashing performs an important function in a visually active quilt like this -- it helps tone down and harmonize blocks that might not play well together if they were sewed together diectly.

The red squares at the junctions of the sashing strips are called cornerstones. You can make sashing with or without cornerstones. I like the cornerstones in this quilt because of the little pop of red they give to the center of the quilt.

Here's how to piece the sashing:

1. Cut five 2" strips of the gray print, then cross-cut the strips into seventeen smaller strips that each measure 2" x 9½".

2. Cut six 2" squares of the red print. Sew a square to one end of six of the gray strips, like this:

3. Lay out the sampler blocks on your work surface as they will be arranged in the finished quilt. Use the quilt diagram at the beginning of the book as a guide.

4. Sew a strip of gray sashing to the right sides of the following eight blocks:

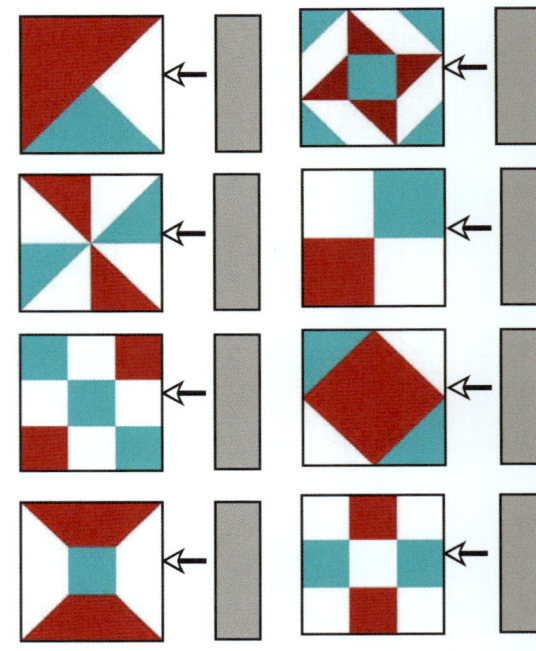

5. Sew the red-and-gray strips to the bottoms of the following six blocks:

6. Sew a gray strip to the bottom edge of the following three blocks:

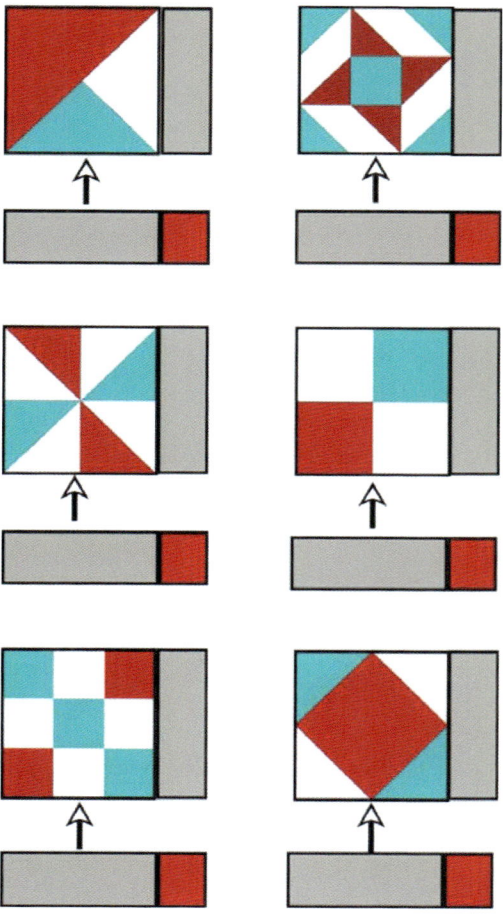

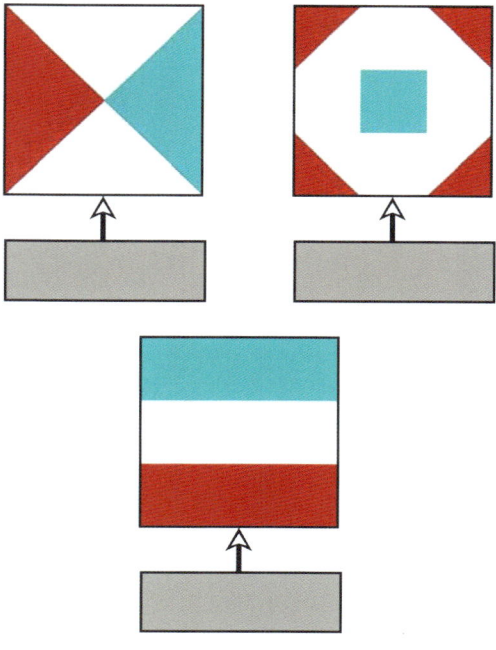

7. Press and square up all the blocks, then lay them out as they are arranged in the quilt pattern at the beginning of the book.

8. Sew the blocks together into rows, starting with the top row and working from left to right along the row. Once you finish the first row, move down to the next row until all the blocks are stitched into rows.

9. Press and square up each row, then sew the rows together, working from the top of the quilt to the bottom.

16/ Quilt Construction: Adding Borders

ADDING BORDERS IS the easiest way to make a quilt larger. Borders also provide a visual frame that enhances the main action in the center of the quilt. The borders on this quilt enlarge it to a comfortable lap quilt size.

Here's how to put borders on your quilt:

1. Once you have sewed together the center section of the quilt, press the center, square it up, and measure it vertically and horizontally, just to make sure the border dimensions I've given here will fit your quilt's actual dimensions.

2. From the gray print, cut two pieces each measuring 4½" x 41" for the side borders, and two pieces each measuring 4½" x 39" for the top and bottom borders.

3. Sew the side borders to the center of the quilt:

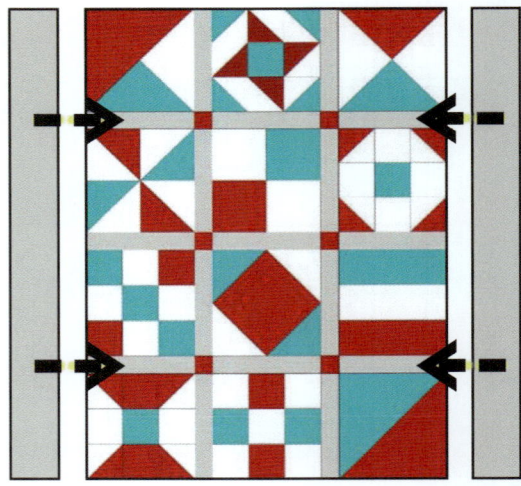

4. Sew the top and bottom borders to the center of the quilt.

17/ Quilt Construction: Finishing the Quilt

Once you have the whole quilt top sewed together, you are near the finish line. There are just three more steps to finishing your quilt: basting, quilting, and putting on the binding. This pattern just gives an overview of the steps involved in finishing the quilt. For complete instructions, see *Quilts for Beginners*.

Basting the Quilt Layers

Basting a quilt means securing the three layers together temporarily until you can sew them together permanently. The easiest way to baste a quilt is to use basting spray.

Make sure the room where you baste is well ventilated, and protect your work surfaces from overspray by putting down a protective cover such as old newspaper or a bed sheet.

1. Cut the batting so it measures 41" x 52" (3" longer and wider than the finished quilt top.)

2. Cut a piece of backing fabric measuring 41" x 52". If your fabric isn't wide enough, cut two pieces the full width of the fabric by 52", and sew them together, then trim down so the pieced backing measures at least 41" x 52".

3. Lay the backing right side down on a flat work surface and tape with blue painter's tape so it is taut and unwrinkled.

4. Spray the backing lightly with basting spray.

5. Unroll the batting layer onto the backing and smooth away any wrinkles.

6. Spray the batting lightly with basting spray.

7. Unroll the quilt top onto the batting layer. Smooth away wrinkles.

Machine Quilting

The simplest way to quilt this sampler is to stitch straight lines along the existing seam lines. This is called stitching in the ditch. You can also quilt the sampler all over in a regular grid pattern. Both of these can be done with the regular straight stitch on any sewing machine.

If you would like the machine quilting to be a bit more decorative, you might try a free-motion stipple on the borders. Free-motion quilting requires a sewing machine that can have the feed dogs dropped out of the way. Here's what a simple stipple looks like:

Putting on the Binding

Binding is a long, double-folded strip of fabric that gets sewed around the outer edge of the quilt to protect the edges from wear. Binding is the last step in making your sampler quilt. Here's what to do:

1. Cut five 2½"-wide strips of the red fabric across the full width of the fabric.

2. Sew the strips together end to end, then trim the seam allowances and press the binding strip in half lengthwise.

3. Sew the binding to the back side of the quilt, then fold it to the front of the quilt and stitch down the folded edge using a straight or decorative stitch on your sewing machine.

18/ Conclusion

I HOPE YOU HAVE enjoyed making this sampler quilt! In fact, I hope you like this pattern so much that you will go on to make many more quilts in the future.

Please Send Me Your Questions

If you have any questions after reading this book, or if there is any way I can help you enjoy quilting more, please do email me for more information. I love to hear from readers. You can reach me at info@QuiltersDiary.com.

And Please Leave a Review

If you find that this book has helped you, I ask you to please post a review for others so they can get started quilting too. To leave a review, just visit the Quilts for Beginners page on Amazon.com and scroll down until you reach the button that says "Write a customer review." Click on the button to add your review.

Thanks for reading, and happy quilting!

19/ About Felicity Walker

I HAVE BEEN QUILTING for nearly 20 years and have made dozens of quilts, but I still remember just what it's like to be taking those first steps toward becoming a quilter.

I probably won't ever enter a quilt in a national show or win prizes for my fancy stitchery, but I love fabric and enjoy making easy quilts for my friends and family. I am always looking for simpler and faster ways to quilt. I have written several best-selling books for quilt lovers.

Now that we've gotten to know each other a little, let's keep in touch.

- Sign up for my free newsletter at my blog, **QuiltersDiary.com**
- Follow me on Pinterest: **Pinterest.com/FelicityWBooks**
- Follow Quilts for Beginners on Facebook: **Facebook.com/QuiltsforBeginners**
- Follow Quilter's Diary on Twitter: **Twitter.com/QuiltersDiary**

More Books for Quilters by Felicity Walker

Quilts for Beginners. Book #1 in the Quilting for Beginners series has everything you need to know to make your first quilts. Includes a detailed, step-by-step photo guide to the basics of quilting – from choosing the right batting, fabric, thread, tools and supplies, to cutting, piecing, basting, quilt-

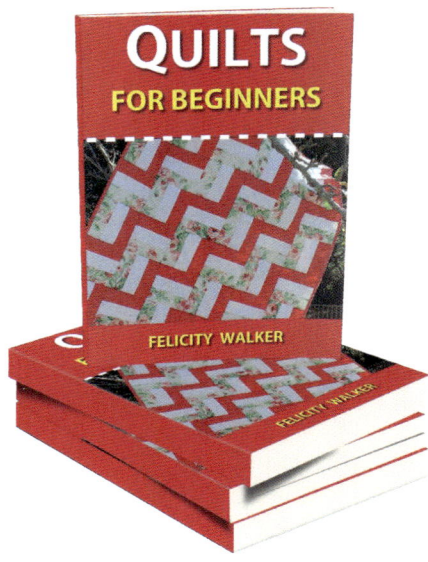

ing, and finishing your quilts. Also includes patterns and complete instructions for three fun and easy quilts. See why other quilters have given this book nearly 60 five-star reviews.

Rag Quilting for Beginners. Book #2 in the Quilting for Beginners series, this book shows you how to make your first rag quilts. Easy enough for absolute beginners, the book includes a complete, step-by-step guide to the basics of rag quilting: choosing fabrics, cutting, sewing, quilting, and finishing a rag quilt, with lots of photos and helpful tips to make everything easy, plus 11 fun and easy rag quilting patterns for beginners, each one with complete photo instructions.

Printable Appliqué Letter and Number Templates. Sew raw-edged appliqué onto quilts, purses, pillows, shirts, dresses, hoodies… you name it! This little book of appliqué alphabet patterns makes it easy to personalize handmade fabric projects with names, words, or dates of special occasions like birthdays, wedding anniversaries, graduations. Includes a complete alphabet of uppercase and lowercase letters, numbers from 0 to 9, and a few commonly used symbols.

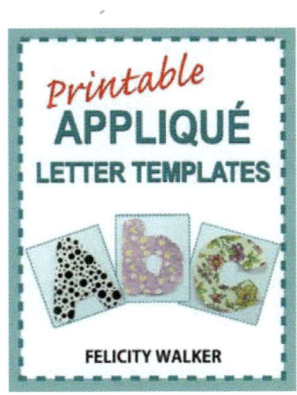

Cats and Quilts Coloring Book. 24 coloring pages featuring beautifully intricate drawings of cats and the quilts they love. Creative relaxation at its best for both adults and children. Perfect for markers, fine-point pens, coloring pencils, or crayons. Each coloring page is blank on the reverse side so colors won't bleed through.

Cats and Quilts 2016 Monthly Calendar. We know who really rules the quilting room! 2016 monthly calendar features twelve cute, clever kitties snuggled up on quilts and in the sewing room. Includes U.S. national holidays. Slim 5½ " x 8½ " size is small enough to tuck into a purse or keep on your desk. January-December 2016.

Printed in Great Britain
by Amazon